For the first time,

platinum-certified singer-songwriter

MARINA

shares her singular observations

of the human heart through poetry;

this collection is essential.

Marina's talent for powerful, evocative song lyrics finds a new outlet in her poetry. Each poem resonates with the same creative melodies and emotional depth that have made her an artistic sensation. Hailed by *The New York Times* for "redefining songs about coming of age, and the aftermath, with bluntness and crafty intelligence," Marina delves even further into trauma, youth, and the highs and lows of relationships in these profound, autobiographical poems to form a collection that transcends the boundaries of music and literature.

PENGUIN LIFE

EAT THE WORLD

MARINA DIAMANDIS is an award-winning, platinum-selling singer-songwriter who burst onto the scene in 2009. She has since released five acclaimed albums: *The Family Jewels* (2010), *Electra Heart* (2012), *FROOT* (2015), *Love + Fear* (2019), and most recently *Ancient Dreams in a Modern Land* (2021), which featured the Ivor Novello–nominated hit "Man's World." All of Marina's records have been accompanied by global, sold-out headline tours with shows at some of the most prestigious venues in the UK and US. A socially engaged figure, she has given an address at the Oxford Union and has an incredibly passionate global fan base. *Eat the World* is her first collection of poetry.

Eat the World

A Collection of Poems by
MARINA DIAMANDIS

life

PENGUIN BOOKS

An imprint of Penguin Random House LLC

penguinrandomhouse.com

A Penguin Life Book

LIBRARY OF CONGRESS CATALOGING-IN-PUBLICATION DATA
Names: Diamandis, Marina, 1985– author.
Title: Eat the world : a collection of poems / Marina Diamandis.
Other titles: Eat the world (Compilation)
Description: [New York] : Penguin Life, 2024. | Summary: "Raw and
moving poems of love, solitude, and the struggles of youth, from fan-
favorite and platinum-certified singer Marina"—Provided by publisher.
Identifiers: LCCN 2024010573 (print) | LCCN 2024010574 (ebook) |
ISBN 9780143138594 (hardcover) | ISBN 9780593512692 (ebook)
Subjects: LCGFT: Poetry.
Classification: LCC PR6104.I18 E28 2024 (print) | LCC PR6104.I18
(ebook) | DDC 823/.92—dc23/eng/20240329
LC record available at https://lccn.loc.gov/2024010573
LC ebook record available at https://lccn.loc.gov/2024010574

Printed in the United States of America
1st Printing

Set in Times New Roman MT Pro Medium
Designed by Dominique Falcone

Contents

Introduction

As I write this, surrounded by moving boxes on a rainy Monday night in LA, on the cusp of entering a new chapter in a new home, I can't help but think about how much my life has changed since I wrote my first poem.

How I came to write a poetry book is fairly curious. One hot summer night, after taking psilocybin, my mind began to write intricate, strange stories drawn from memories old and recent. At first I thought they were songs, so I tried to box them into their usual structures, but they refused to obey. They seemed to want to expand and unfurl into their own shapes, so I put them aside and laid them to rest. A few weeks later, I realized that they were poems, not songs, and from that moment onward, my love for this new medium was born. I had found a new way to confess, process, and play with the past.

Writing is a way to remember and also a way to forget, to let go. Since I was 20 years old, I have used it as a way to alchemize pain. To explore wounds so that I can heal them, to understand them intimately so that I can let them go. My love for writing is intrinsically linked to its magical ability to ignite significant chapters of self-growth. It's an invisible thread that connects me back to my true self, an internal North Star that leads me back to a place where truth, power, and freedom reside.

In this age of social media dominance, where we present our happiest, most successful selves online, we are left with increasingly fewer spaces to let the murkier versions of ourselves breathe. The scared, insecure parts; the self-doubting, lonely corners that we find too shameful or ugly to present around others. Writing poetry has helped me to uncover and integrate the parts of myself I'd tried hard to hide. The feelings of loneliness, shame, and alienation that had long fueled my music found a new place to breathe and exist in peace.

I hope this book brings solace to those who need it. Sometimes, it can feel like no one in the world feels the same way that you do. But the truth is, many of us experience the same challenges, just at different times in life.

Connection is never far away. Words are portals that lead us into new worlds of resonance, wisdom, and healing. I hope this book can be a friend to you as it has been for me.

MARINA

JANUARY 2024

Eat the World

Starlight
Water
Space   Fresh
Air

i can't live where i'm from
it hurts too much
so i put my hand up
and volunteer

to be an eternal sapling.

ready to be transplanted
at a moment's notice
into a pot of warm soil
hoping that this time

my roots will grow.

that
i'll
be
nourished
by

star light,

water,   space,

fresh air

that
wasn't
polluted
at
the
source

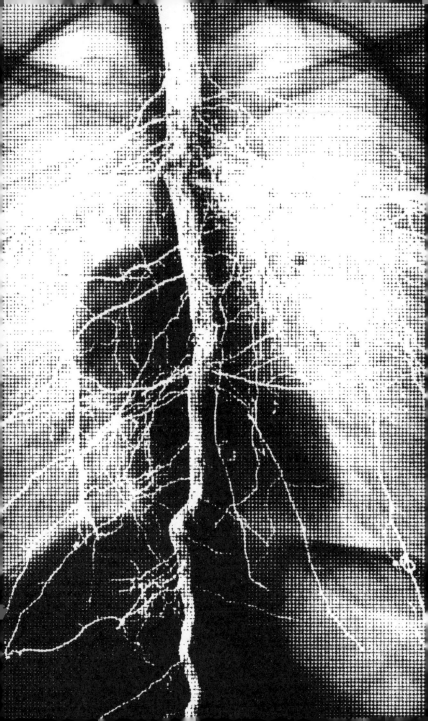

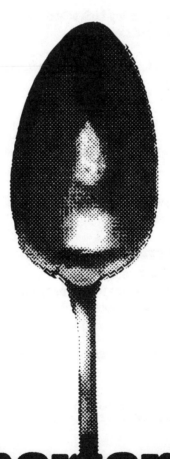

Aspartame

I arrived here at 20, rail thin in a polka-dot
 dress,   tooth enamel dissolved by stomach acid

I was banking on my high school sweetheart
to be a source of love

An injection for a supply I'd been mercilessly
cut off from

                        It didn't work.

In the time we'd spent apart, he'd become a surfer
up in San Luis Obispo

and had developed a penchant for getting high
at 5 in the morning

I spent my time with him mainly:

        a) not eating
        b) checking the status of my hip bones
        c) hiding from his alpha roommates

I'd wander around town cosplaying as a girl next door
hitting up TJ Maxx

like a normal American girl
        in a normal American world

Far from   a singing career,   close to
                                                    failure

I was a

        bulimic
     college

       dropout

with

     no family.

Except there was family.

My Mum, who I called in desperation
to book my plane ticket home.

Things went sour fast and my high school sweetheart
turned to aspartame dust

I took the train to Hollywood (like a cliché) and rode
the Amtrak like I was in the lap of luxuré

Relieved to have escaped the tension of a reunion gone
bad.

Hollywood Boulevard smelled like the apocalypse and
the pale winter light added to my feeling of

dissociation

of not being real anymore
of life being a numb game.
I could've died and not felt anything.

I spent my days visiting emo stores on
Melrose, dodging drug addicts on trains
and shopping at Forever 21

On my last night I caught my reflection, a silver light
bouncing off ribs protruding crudely from my back

It was then that I realized the jig was up.

My plan to be thin hadn't worked.
I didn't make him love me.

Years later, we met again at the Roosevelt Hotel,
two old friends sharing the same soul connection

we'd had in high school. He told me when he'd seen
the "Hollywood" video he'd felt sick.

Because I'd achieved my dreams. Because I wasn't a lunatic.

And somehow it healed a forgotten part of me.
He was the only one I'd ever told about my dreams.

I was no longer a victim. I had been redeemed.
No longer a dropout. He had seen me succeed.

And finally, I wasn't who I was at seventeen anymore.

Pain Eraser

the things
i need
to write about

are the things
i'm scared
to write about

lest they blow
up my life

and everything
i tried
so hard to

save
    mend
        bury
            heal

Death by Panamera

I have a private list
I tell no one about

of terrible things
that might never happen to me.

A supernova inventory
of star-sharp fears

that explodes and expands
when things get out of hand

Top of the list:

1) Careening off a cliff

when I am 56
in a 911 Carrera

2) Having no friends

Being forgotten in the end

(Would death be avoided
if I drove a Panamera?)

3) Depending on strangers

Growing older alone
Having kids

Being trapped
in a life I don't own

4) Remaining child-free

and living in peace
but never knowing love

as dazzling or deep

5) Is the strangest one on the list

I'm scared to be happy
I'm scared that I'll miss

being sad
Even though

I so want
to be free

But I've known it so long
I don't want it to leave

and I guess that's the end
of a list I don't need

I'm searching for proof
of time
Searching for the scent I smell
in Athens
Soaked into city walls marble floors
kafenia and
the skin of centenarians.

Searching for proof of a society
that existed
   Pre lip fillers
             and pre butts lifted

    but

                         it's   gone .

10,000 years wiped off the hard drive
eradicated by
a human drive to survive at any cost
All civilizations
start from zero anyway so why would it be
any different in

LA?

Proof is torn down here and quickly replaced
by

shiny white boxes, flat featureless shrines
homages to
linear anodyne lines
It is a plastic Parthenon, an ode
to its ancient ancestors
Mickey and Minnie
Psychedelic pink skies render films obsolete

whilst valleys

lie mutely locked under concrete
below ancient trails
of the Tongva tribe and their lifeline rivers
that now run dry

And finally I find
proof of time.

It's faint, like a hint of jasmine in the dark
hanging low, indiscreet, tiny tremor at your feet
Gatorades chugged
in the heat E numbers bouncing like a Jeep,
as walrus bones shake down the street from CVS
to Pinkberry
A tectonic heartbeat

— proof of time, trying to speak

Fizz

Much as you try,

       the thin fizz of

              desperation

                     is a giveaway.

You are not a natural.

             You are a trier.

Trying is your way

          Going for broke

                 Only plan A

        Your history is such

you will always find a way

                 You can adapt to anything

       Yet you still feel ashamed

         to be a trier

Smoothness of Money

You remind me of British summertime

lush lawns, green countryside,

M&S sandwiches, eating lunch outside

> with your glossy, perfect family, so kind they made me nervous.

Golden retrievers, a farmhouse, a pool

The security money could bring.

A life that could have been mine

Lies that could have been yours

> I was 21, an amateur and lacking the self-worth to choose better.

We were cartoon versions of an atomic

bomb button, pressing up against each other

until one of us blew. You hid your weakness

behind haircuts and emo music

m y s p a c e   p r o f i l e s

and webcams you spoke to girls

called "jaymie <3" on

I hid behind thrift clothes, binge-purge cycles

and bad hair dyes. I picked up a microwave

meal for you on our 2nd date and thought it was love.

*"These are the **best** years of your life"*

You had a world I wasn't allowed into.

I was rough around the edges, yet to be popular

and you were embarrassed of me.

I didn't have the   smoothness of m o n e y   like you did.

But one day I would

And you would hate that I'd earned it.

Butterflies

i laugh easily

i wish i didn't.

It comes from

teetering on the edge
of someone else's desires

It comes from

Complying

not wanting to cause discomfort to others

Fuck others.

Why do i have to bear
the weight of the discomfort?

Let's sit in this crevice of awkward silence together.

So you can absorb how you

stained my soul

crushed my spirit

and ability to form sentences.

i wish i talked slower.

let the words linger

and be born

in full form

but instead they skitter

like butterflies
in a storm.

i stutter when i'm tired.

How to speak surely, though?

when i'm not sure
if you are listening

School of Life

Remember when i talked at the school of life and in the car home how you made me cry right before i flew to new york on a red-eye gumball-red eyes can't count how many times fresh pink swollen face tear ducts salinate what a waste—you couldn't appreciate my mind but then again they say the connections we create are mirrors of our ways snapshot our internal state and i've been on enough dates now to know this to be true you need to first be the right person to bring the right person to you.

Million Tiny Knives

I spent seven years feeling
like my skin was inside out

Plagued by panic attacks
the body found ways

to communicate
and detonate
the truth

Deeply unhappy and deeply
in love I couldn't see the killer

but I could smell the blood.

"something is very sick in my life"

Couldn't put a finger on it
long enough to make a case

No amount of evidence
was enough to persuade

Him of disconnection.
Him of self-denial
Him of severed instincts
Unwittingly on trial

Karmic threads that extend
my comprehension of their

lineage stitched themselves
tighter, trapping me inside

a dress that wasn't mine to wear.

I turned a blind eye at first
thought they'd stop once they knew

we were in love

They didn't.

They wanted incest.
Wanted family.
Wanted blood.

Skin a clammy pallor
two Victorian doll eyes

belying no emotion and
every emotion all the time

One glance my way felt like
a million tiny knives, I could

never quite explain why it
sent shivers down my spine

"At first they felt like scratches
I didn't want to make a fuss
until one morning I woke up
and I was covered in my blood"

My dreams began to die
by a million tiny cuts

crisscrossing softly over time
noughts 'n crossing through the

night until the day that I decided:

Enough.

Cut to today in LA life,
I saw their first victim last night

We hallelujah'd and high 5'd

"Congrats, you made it out alive"

and the strangest thing I learned
is that the dangers in my life

were so much worse than all my fears
worse than someone who could connive

Abusive, sick, violent, illegal. Somebody wild,
wounded and sad.

And though it won't mean much to others, it
disturbed the peace I had

because I'd felt it all along and I had seen it from the
start:

A serial killer mind hiding inside a darker art.

Out of Production

Two years after the split, I realize: there will be no
new memories.

Now that pain has faded, I find myself protecting
the good ones. Taking them out of their boxes and
polishing them. Like well-loved shoes no longer in
production.

Your favorites will be different from mine. Different
holidays, different special nights. That are solely ours
and will only ever be. (Not even the home surveillance
on your street can touch these.)

Sometimes I think morbid little thoughts, like

> *"One day one of us
> will wake to news that
> the other has died"*

and we might feel shock—or total surprise. We might
tell a spouse and conceal our sadness with a casual
tone used for tales of blandness.

I wish our end were different, all lovers wish the same.
But as I departed pain you entered it like a t r a i n

and encountered a station you'd avoided your whole
life.

In the end we found our ways

We both built something new.

Am I allowed to still think of you?

Or should I ask

you to depart

my heart

so it can be reclaimed

and new memories can be made

Soft Warning

I love her but she makes me nervous

Impermanence permeates
every valley, every canyon

A soft warning:

"you cannot have me forever"

I love her but she makes me nervous

I know it's unsustainable to live here
—cruel to take her last drops of water

for our swimming pools

(I love her but she makes me *nervous*)

So I wait until it's time to vacate
to a new place with less threat

of droughts, wildfires, earthquakes—
But what if I don't find another LA?

I love her . . . But she makes me <u>nervous</u>

To put down roots, though I so badly want to,
but I fear they'll be cut up and snatched if I do

Is it predictable of me to fall in love with a
place built on shaky ground?

Factory Settings

my relationships hang
like broken spider-
webs in the sun

blue silver holes
gape like spotlights
when the wind blows

do i try to mend
the old web or build
a brand-new one?

i'm tired of spinning, though / tired of keeping afloat /
no life buoys left / on the inside of my boat

why do i make myself start over? /
how is this my life / how do i override

my factory settings

Land of Limbs

Incubator of the future

Apocalyptic playground
You must love novelty
to live here

Cynics do not survive
They move away
to cooler climes
Leave their bile behind

on sidewalks to sizzle
and evaporate into

clouds of vaporized dreams

Town of transplants
City of saplings
Land of amputated limbs

Millions of orphaned
legs hands feet looking
to rejoin their bodies

Searching to be sewn
back onto where
they belong

Sometimes I think:

If you weren't born
here you need to be
lost to live here

Or comfortable being
separated from your

organ of origin

I know everyone
writes about LA
but I am one of
her children now too

No longer an orphan
I've been adopted
No longer lost
I've been co-opted

By a

Town of transplants
A city of saplings and a
Land of amputated limbs

Beautiful/Evil

a plane cut through sky
candy apple red

a virgin atlantic–themed
bird overhead

the most beautiful/evil
thing i'd ever seen

i felt sad for the birds
at the top of the tree

i only ever noticed them
when i was high

my life was quite good
but i wanted to die

had no clear reasons
to keep being alive

life felt both easy
and hard to survive

Billionaire's Beach

Master of theater
It has performed
for millennia

Never missed a scene
No entrance fee
required

Not even on
Billionaire's
Beach.

A crack of explosion
is deftly performed
when two waves meet,

crash hard, locking
horns, like an
ancient gunshot

and then it passes
So nonchalant
it rescinds, advances

Prehistoric and new
Violent and calm
All at the same time

It reminds me that
it fights against itself,
like humans do.

Tiny joys, archaic
tragedies, oil slick woes
climate change maladies

The ocean doesn't care
because it knows it
will be there

forever.

Until it splits into
a trillion tears
cried from the

cornea of God,
propelled back
into time

The ocean laughs
at sea scum. It is

a billion times

more powerful
than Tesla and
Silicon Valley

More powerful
than oil spills
plastic bags

and sewer filth
from Venice.
Fuzzy fizzy

white, glossy
foamy frothy
sparkling surf,

where fish flirt
across the stage
of another wave

And I stay
on the sand
so far away

Half enraptured
half in love
half in awe

and so afraid

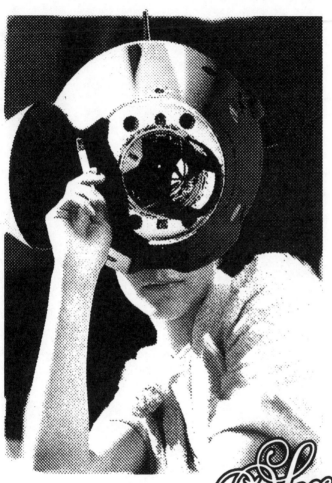

Sex ROBOT

I want a hot boy!

OK I mean,

Who's not 28

Is that so much to ask ?

Who doesn't tell jokes
that don't make me laugh
Or point out my flaws
to conceal his wrath

No stylist in September
nor nurse in November
who grew up on porn
and forgot to be tender

Treating women like rag dolls
to be dominated
by sex robots with six-packs
that came pre-inflated

Inflation is great
until comes the recession
When it's clear it's not love
—it's not even obsession

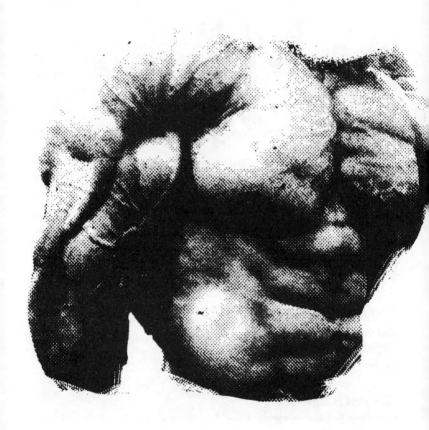

I hear the air hiss from his biceps—confession
Python discarding me like a skin—a lesson
I'm too fragile for even this teenage rejection

But anyhow, anyhow
Everyone's married now
Nobody's going out
I'm the last girl in town

of my kind
I don't mind
but it would be nice to find

Somebody solid,
who's actually there
No hot-air balloon
prone to rogue g u s ts o f   ai r

I'm still on the carousel,
alone at the fair

No sex robots, please!
Just a
giant
teddy
bear

Moon Rock

We have the same holes
in us, like moon rock.

From afar, we look bright
The sun makes our gaps glitter

But up close, we have the same holes

Our silhouettes lock into
single file when we hug

Like pieces of Swiss cheese
cut from the same block

And I get that sinking feeling
(even though you're hot)

That we can't give each
other what we haven't got

We feel worse together,
somehow more incomplete

Holes deeper than deep.

And we part ways wondering
why we're emptier than before

You and I are like moon rock.

Lost
Cold
Alien
Discrete

Stolen from another galaxy

Looking for a slice of brie,
for what we need is melted cheese

Night Surfing

You like

night surfing
driving ducatis
911 carreras
and working 15
hours in a row

Thrill seeker
lover of flesh
hot-blooded man
no one can impress

except me

because

I already have
everything I need

and because

the things
you love
scare me

I am unbendable now

You ask if
poetry is dead
Your questions
linger in my head

You are a good
question asker

Effervescent
like my father

But I protect
myself now
as if I were
my daughter

I'm no lamb to the
slaughter I can
no longer falter

Cannot trick
my heart to
see you as a
seed to water

But you're joyous
and an expert in
drawing dreams
out of dirt

on the coast of
Malibu to the
secret place
you took me to

that only had
an outside loo
Nothing for miles
but baby blue

You're macho
and you're fragile
Egoic, fit and
agile from all

the night surfing
(which vexed me)
But I can't explain

why that's sexy

FOUR Seasons

No broken families
at the four seasons

    just me on the beach
    a discrete anomaly

No broken families
at the four seasons

    just thin sullen teens
    from Texas on holiday

    It feels good to witness
    these families up close

    as if i'm an alien
    quietly taking notes

No broken families
at the four seasons

    just couples teamed up
    together till they die

No broken families
at the four seasons

    just jade-colored pools
    and periwinkle skies

They talk about golf
like they're actually happy
last year in St. Kitts
this year they're in Maui

Their voices flow by me
with lightness and ease
Calling out for their kids
—a touching receipt

No broken families
at the four seasons

just mahogany dads
turning brown into pink

An unusual shade that
reminds me of Christmas
or a Thanksgiving ad
with roast turkey skin

No broken families
at the four seasons

just care and belonging
that is tender to see

And i can't help but wonder,
even though i feel lucky,
if life had been different,
could that have been me?

I could've been a woman
with a windbreaker on!
Thick, shiny black hair
tied back in a bun

Discreet diamond studs
that winked in the sun
a child in each hand
Oh, see how they run!

I guess what I'm saying
is i'd like to taste
a slice of security
one piece of the cake

what are the ingredients?
what if i can't bake?

maybe no one can
we all just have to pretend

i put down my pen
my heart starts to ache

no longer feeling
like i'm on a holiday

i say   to myself

"that's   e nough

for today

you can't have it all
life is not
a buffet"

Merman

I saw you trying to get
into the tower of love

An underwater castle
that lay in the middle of

your life.

You peered through the

glass, face pressed up close,

like a child left out of a game.

Your serious expression
broke my heart, it was

the same one you wore
in every photograph

on your Hinge profile.

You said you "loved to have fun"
but I never saw you smile

widely or freely

You tried once when inside
me but it came out smug

like an inside joke
I couldn't be a part of

You were a good person
but not a good partner

Locked in your own world
hiding underwater

Protecting yourself

from
love

The Sparkling CLAM

🐚 Time is a precious commodity
when you know yourself too well

Know when you know better
I knew from the start this time

The charm came too soon.

I liked being adored but

when he cast his net

I never
    got caught

Instead I
slipped free
and escaped his night trawl
Fell tumbling

d

o

w

n

to a jet-black
ocean floor

I shut my shell up tight
every opening a risk to
my soft gray center

*Sssssssssss*and sifted across my seabed
There was safety in solitude
"i can't stay shut forever"

I don't need to.
    I just must avoid
        the fishermen
        the sailors
        the soldiers
        the boys
    who will
        suck out my pearls
        peel off my shell
        boil my body
& call me dinner

Slowly   but   surely
        I became a sparkling clam

spending days in sun rays
on virgin gold sand

Elegant and violent
strengthened by escape

from the butchers above
who knew nothing of love

Just the ritual massacre

     "Bait Scrape Suffocate"

One Friday night I thought

Is death really worse
than eternal loneliness?

Is the danger of damage
better than its absence?

I spend my days in silence
at the bottom of the sea

Cool dark and clean
Now safe and serene

Yet I yearn
to o pe n up
and return
to sea level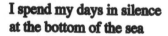

I don't want the same anymore

I am aware of

how comfortable

I am being ignored

how comfortable

I am living

on a tightrope

waiting for a man's

attention to somersault

and land on me.

More disconcerting

is when he

communicates frequently

Trains of texts

arriving curiously

on time

Instinctively I feel

overwhelmed

retreat into a corner

the rules

of the game

interrupted.

I have high tolerance

for low contact

which attracts

ramshackle types;

the emotionally rusty

with brains like boxes

of nuts and bolts

Pairs of magnets

simultaneously repelling

and attracting each other

Stuck

in our

own tragicomedy.

I don't want to be prey

for old patterns

I've read books, taken courses

gone to therapy

Please believe me, God

when I say:

I don't want the same anymore.

Tiny Leopards

Leopard-print belly
Sun rays sear
through caramel fur

Spots out! Dots out!

IT'S BART

Tiny face and jaunty gait
Eyes glow green like
fresh peeled grapes

Always keen quite
rarely mean mischievous
mouth cheerful and clean

Never been haughty
like his sister
The Benevolent Diva:

BETSY JEAN

She's wild and shy
A jungle queen
Everglade eyes
Hunting sunbeams

Often felt but rarely
seen just like a storm
she sets her scene

Half toffee fluff
Eyes full of spark
She hunches down
and makes her mark

By Kung Fu Fighting
in the air with
hummingbirds

She's Fred Astaire!
She's Ginger Rogers
in her world, a VIP
life kind of girl

And I her humble
paparazzo follow her
loyally everywhere

Hoping for access,
information
Does she love me?
Does she care?

Hotel Riche

The peace I feel in the sky
is unparalleled

I don't mean on a plane
but on the 52nd floor

of the Four Seasons
Hotel Philadelphia

The hot hush of sound
as I exit the ground

Zooming out from bellboys
smiling miles from the town

Whizzing up through night
like hell's angels in flight

Nothing touches me now
Just encase me in clouds

Encase me in a town where
I mean nothing to anyone

I'm alone and at home
Like a mossed rolling stone

I am safe in this place
Being Madeline for a day

Playing hide, evaporate
disappear and escape

Denominator

all the people
i rely on

are paid
i feel the urge

to run away
to say:

"i'm not sure
who cares"

and no one's
to blame

it's a job
for lovers

for daughters
and brothers

for grandmas
and fathers

and sisters
and mothers

"hi!"

a severed
hand waving

to no one
ready to detach

and jump
ship to italy

if i'm going
to be alone

i might as well
live prettily

close to lemon
groves and far

from LA
where they make

you pay for your
own placenta

don't think i
don't know

i'm the common
denominator

i can't run
from myself

not ever again
life is the canvas

my thoughts are the paint
words are my brushes

so i watch what i say
if i want a new life

then i need a new brain

Pink Elephant

What if LA is becoming a sad city for me?   What if I don't meet anyone?
Where will I run?   Where will I go?
Can somebody save me?   You're not meant to say that, though.

You're meant to say

"Only I can save myself!"

The pressure to fill weekends   To not look alone
Builds up over time   Pulls you taut like a yo-yo

Until one day you realize your only choice is to surrender to the
elephant in the room:

The sheer aloneness of living

Hello, have we met?
I've avoided you my whole life.
I've seen you at parties
In supermarket aisles
I pretend not to see you
We never lock eyes

Loneliness

u r   m y   k r y p t o n i t e

Lurking in the back   I keep a lid on you for fear
you'll burst out of the trash   like Oscar the Grouch.

I remind myself on tough nights

That loneliness and truth   >   company and lies

That some emotions wait decades to express themselves.

That difficult feelings are as valuable as joyful ones.

And that my resistance to loneliness is what kept me the loneliest.

1,000 Black Nights

Rage is a place kept
permanently locked

Who will give me the
key to this city?

What ribbon of therapy
do I have to cut?

I am so out of touch
with its rough texture

I run my fingers along its
city walls and stall

as I consider trespassing.

I conjured it recently
So struck by its force

I saw stars from a
thousand black nights

A result of my neurons
pressing weeping black

wounds downdowndown
into my nervous system

just for them to seep out
in other ways

"Depression is anger turned inward"

Terrifying screams
surprisingly cut from

my own vocal cords
begin to reverberate

Like an AI version
of how it would sound

if I were actually, genuinely
deeply enraged

I am rageful
I have my reasons

but it doesn't scare
me anymore

Because I know
rage is not forever

It passes

It has purpose

and to deny it

is to keep it alive

E-motion

Why is it hard to accept emotions? Why do

we twist them into shapes they are not?

They only re-form the shape in which

they're born when we're not looking.

Why deny, resist and list them instead of

letting them rest inside our bodies

What am I scared of? That I'll die of

discomfort or that they'll last forever?

20 seconds.

Apparently that's how long

it takes for an emotion to be felt

We store them in boxes called illness

and backache, instead of letting them

move so they can take up space to

one day eventually—poof—evaporate

Their purpose is to move, be felt

as energy in motion.

We don't choose their arrival

But we choose our response, so we might

as well greet them and treat them like friends.

Inner Peace & Other Lies

Control is kryptonite

uncertainty a parasite

Nothing surprises me anymore

Life feels like

a flat black river

unmoving and unclear

In unnatural ways

I spoke to Marcela on

Zoom the other day

Said *"I hold myself hostage*

to my to-do lists"

Underneath compulsion

lies a quest for balance

as a prize, a dog-eared

lotto ticket for

inner peace & other lies

Because the source of

the disorder has always

been on my inside

A gnawing fear bad things

will happen if I stop

holding on so tight

Heavy Metals

A crack in the back bleeds black

      Heavy metals in my cells
weigh me down

      In order to change shape
I need to let go

      Detoxify my blood
of her tart red anger

      that runs ribbons, snakes, bows
through every organ, vein, bone

      before nesting dormant in my heart.

It sits densely. Privately. Uncontrollable black bomb.

Waits to explode out
      And spray frayed body parts

Across skies and stars
      Until shards of my heart

Puncture the planets.

Shame makes it
      Cower and condense

Further inward
      "Stay small, hard and static"

But the less I move,
    the less I'm able to change.

I remain locked in form,
    like a soldier in march

So obedient to the past.
    I'm scared of you, anger

and your bulletproof cast.

    What does it take to
make you break?

    Words?

Words.

A white flag at last.

Blockbuster

Your life runs like a movie

Kidnappings killings starvation
before you even left the womb.

How to describe this lineage?
This deep drive to survive

to change your destiny
to make it out alive.

This tapestry of hardship
embroidered with fear

offers few pockets of
relatability to grip on to

It only finds home in the
context of a blockbuster

where we can detach ourselves
and marvel at how all this

could have happened to
one person.

Marie Kondo

I found your old letters
whilst Marie Kondo–ing

my house and a veil of
doom descended over me

They did not "spark joy."

Paperweights lowered
themselves carefully into

my heart. Opening Pandora's
box seemed pointless

But I did it anyway
and read the story of us.

What I learned is that
you are neither

devil nor angel,
hell nor heaven,
careless nor careful.

Poisoned arrows shot years
ago now seemed comedic

as if they were thrown
by tiny laughing cupids.

I still look for ways to
fill up the old wound

Too deep to heal fully
Too small for ICU

I guess I always thought
you didn't love me enough

I never considered you might
love me too much

Broken Heart Syndrome

It slides through like the last slip of sand in an hourglass. A realization almost absurd in its simplicity

"I can have a beautiful life"

Togetherness, closeness, dependence is possible. A different outcome is possible.

To create a beautiful life I have to imagine it first.

Like a poem or a painting, I need to draw my own outline.

Believe in its beauty before I can see it with my own eyes.
Believe I can have it all.
That I can be lucky in multiple ways.

I'm not sure why it took me longer than most, but I am undeterred.
The nature of my path made me robust and enduring.

I'm going to dream a new dream, instead of seeing the same nightmare.
Dream a new scene where I pick what part I play.

The first step is to stop identifying with past versions of myself.

The one where I'm a lone wolf and can't trust another.
The one where I don't need the help of my mother.

And the one where the wound has long healed but

the child lives on as if broken at the center

When really, the child is now an adult

independent, fortunate and free

to create a new future

Eclipse

Change didn't come quickly.

It came in slowly, tentatively,

like a child on their first day at school.

Its foundation sifted in with the wind each night,

grain by grain, layer by layer. Until one day I woke up

and realized I had walls. I had somehow become a

home for myself.

The roots of trauma, now yellowed and withered, fell

away in the wind.

The past no longer hot gossip I exploded onto friends.

And the men

I met were

different.

Gentle, complete

beings who knew

themselves well.

No need to impress

or prove their wealth

I realized I did it.

I'd built my own life

And I did it without

having to be a

mother or a wife

Slowly but surely

my desire to change

had finally eclipsed

my desire to stay the same.

Behemoth

All the tears, sweat, blood
that went into building you

Terrazzo from Italy
ceramic slipper baths

Yellow zellige tiles
happy like California

to erase the deep blues
from our bitter aftermath

Walls dabbed carefully
in soft roman clay

in deep earthy tones
to elicit "OK"

To elicit inner peace
clear skin, good health

To evoke that fine line
between nature and wealth

Sparkling cyan pool
that I swam in 10 times

Teak loungers I so rarely
relaxed out upon

"There's not enough sun"

"Takes one day to heat it"

"This canyon is shady . . ."

"THIS CANYON'S A POND!"

Had something to do
with the bones, dna

The structure, the heart
the lack of proper veins

I know we don't fit but
you're hard to give away

You were once so adored
You were something I saved

All the dreams I un-birthed
All of our unlived lives

And the real sunken cost
of just how hard I had tried

The idea still stings
But I let the house win

Behemoth of my heart
Goodbye is the right thing
♥

I want my old life back
but it's gone.

I've metamorphosed
into a wonky

butter fly

Wings don't work
Feet feel frazzled

I creep back into
my cocoon
hoping

it's not too
late to
transform.

(Universe, let me off this one time?)

I've been wrapped
in this film
of gray

for too long.
Every year
since birth

a new layer
has emerged.
So protective

at first, it now
feels like a

curse

Most butterflies get
free at 21,
23

I'm 37 now and
the gray layers
run deep.

Mummy-like, weigh

me down, keep me

buried underground

I've been so scared
you see, to
be free

For fear I cause an
earthquake to
other insects.

For the beauty of a butterfly
is seen as a threat to those
who have never *truly flown*.

Never felt clean   wind on iridescent   wings

Never tasted the nectar
that summer   flowers bring

So to keep them safe
I have kept myself
hidden

(It can't be too late?)
As my layers here thicken
my breath starts
    to quicken

And panic -   stricken,
I sense my structure
    closing in

Life watches me pass by.

This cocoon will be
a casket if I don't
start living soon

If I don't escape
this room, so
I start to

rap my wings on
my honeycombed
tomb

A quiet promise in my
mind: *"I will free
myself soon"*

Eventually decay

s p   l   i   t   s

my walls
wide   open

The rot has got
me angry
hot

*(Becoming a butterfly
     is not what I thot)*

🦋 Metamorphosis
🦋 awaits every being
🦋 in the end

If you don't break your
cocoon soon, life will do
it for you, friend

These days when I see
butterflies float
effortlessly by

I know exactly what it takes
to grow the wings
they need to fly

They make it look so easy
twinkling metallic
in the sky

But I know the pain of
changing shape, I know
the exact price

Now I can see, to truly
live, parts of me
had to die

To be reborn
again, again,

a   better   butterfly